MW01067813

The Land of Shapes

Volume 1:
Circle Adopts a Pet

Land of Shapes Vol. 1: Circle Adopts a Pet
Copyright © 2013 by Colin McConnell. All rights reserved.
First Print Edition: August 2013

This book is best suited for children between the age of 2 and 10, but can still be enjoyed by someone of any age.

No part of this book may be reproduced, scanned, or distributed in any printed or electronic form without permission.

This is a work of fiction. Names, characters, places, and incidents either are the product of the author's imagination or are used fictitiously, and any resemblance to locales, events, business establishments, or actual persons—living or dead—is entirely coincidental.

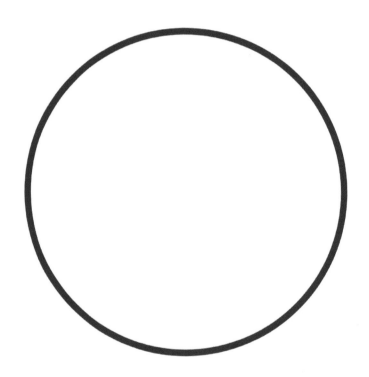

Circle

Today, Circle woke up in a very good mood.

He was heading to the park for the pet adoption day.

Circle was on a mission to adopt a dog. But, he had to find the one that was the best fit for him.

The first dog Circle met had way too many wrinkles. So, he decided to keep looking.

He walked a bit and came upon a second dog. This dog was too hairy. Circle knew he would be picking a lot of hair up around his house if he chose this dog.

When Circle came to the third dog, he thought it was just a little too small for him.

When Circle came upon the fourth dog, he thought he was seeing a furry tree trunk. This dog was just way too tall. His house was too small to fit a dog that huge.

When Circle came to the fifth dog he saw, he had a really good feeling.

He said, "Hi," with a big smile on his face. But, the dog just kept walking.

What's that noise coming from the behind the tree? As Circle got closer he saw the sixth dog snoring. Should he try and wake him up?

The seventh dog had way too much energy for Circle to handle. It bounced and bounced all over the park.

The eighth dog was barking so loud that Circle decided to move on in hopes of finding a pet that was just right.

The ninth dog wasn't a dog at all. It was a cat. Circle was sad because he couldn't find the right dog for him.

Then as he was walking home...

...Circle looked down and saw a dog looking up at him with a smile on his face and tail wagging.

Circle didn't think he would ever find the perfect pet. Now Circle had to choose the perfect name. Can you help Circle think of a name?

Activities with Circle
Place your finger on the arrow and slowly trace the dotted lines.

Help Circle get to his new dog. Get the sleepy dog to the alarm clock, and direct the barking dog to his bowl of food.

Place your finger on the arrow and slowly trace the lines around Circle three times.

The next two pages sum up the journey Circle took to find his new dog. The task will be for the child to find all the characters from the story and describe to you what was done with each character. This task will assist with visual exploration by scanning the visually stimulating pages to find the dogs as well as sequencing, visualization, and comprehension. Have the child(ren) find the dogs in order as they appeared in the story and then explore their mental pictures to tell the story of how Circle came to adopt his new friend. You can also call out different things in the picture and have them point it out. Change the order every time you read it to change it up. Have fun!

Adopt a Pet.

PARK

If you enjoyed this story, be sure to check out the next installment in the Land of the Shapes series:

The Land of
Shapes
Vol 2

COOKING WITH
Pierre
and
Square
Episode 1: Sugar Cookies

by: Colin McConnell

Smile BIG
Smile often!